Only the best quality resources for teachers, parents, and students!

PHILLIPS
- Resources -

Contents

Visit
phillipsresources.co.uk
for hundreds more of
the best revision
resources

Use code: 'PR20' for 20% off at checkout ;)

Coastal Landscapes

8 Mark Questions:

Explain the influence of climate change on raised beaches **[8]**

Explain how physical factors influence the coastal landscape system **[8]**

Explain how flows of energy and material influence geomorphic processes of a coastal landscape **[8]**

Explain how a sediment cell can be viewed as a system **[8]**

Explain how geology influences coastal landscape systems **[8]**

Explain the formation of a spit **[8]**

Explain the role of flows of energy in the formation of a tombolo **[8]**

16 Mark Questions:

'Geology is the most significant influence on coastal landscapes.' To what extent do you agree with this statement? **[16]**

Using a case study, assess the relative importance of the different physical factors influencing the landscape of a low energy coastline **[16]**

'The changes caused by human activity in coastal landscapes are always negative.' Discuss. **[16]**

Using a case study, assess the extent to which landforms within a low energy coastal environment are inter-related **[16]**

Using a case study, assess the reasons for economic development taking place in a coastal landscape being used by people **[16]**

Short Questions:

1. Study **Table 1** which shows mean rates of shoreline retreat for 6 areas of the UK.

Mean rate of shoreline retreat (m/yr)	0.7	0.3	1.1	1.6	0.9	0.5

Table 1: Mean rate of shoreline retreat for 6 areas of the UK

(a) Calculate the median for the data shown in **Table 1**. You must show your working. **[2]**

(b) Calculate the interquartile range for the date shown in **Table 1**. You must show your working. **[4]**

2. Study **Table 2** which shows inputs and outputs of sediment for a beach in Devon, UK, during 2023

		Summer	Winter
Input (m³)	Fluvial Deposition	56	34
	Cliff erosion	38	100
	Beach nourishment	45	0
Output (m³)	Marine erosion	25	72
	Longshore drift	79	125

Table 2: Inputs and outputs for Devon beach, UK, 2023

(a) Calculate the sediment budget for each season shown in **Table 2**. You must show your working. **[2]**

Glaciated Landscapes

8 Mark Questions:

Explain the role of flows and stores in the formation of an erratic. **[8]**

Explain how a glacier can be viewed as a system. **[8]**

Explain the influence of climate change on kames. **[8]**

Explain how geology influences glaciated landscape systems. **[8]**

Explain the formation of a corrie. **[8]**

Explain one geomorphic process involved in the formation of one periglacial landform. **[8]**

16 Mark Questions:

'The changes caused by human activity in glaciated landscapes are always negative.' Discuss. **[16]**

Using a case study, assess the extent to which landforms within a valley glacier system are inter-related. **[16]**

'Geology is the most significant influence on glaciated landscapes.' To what extent do you agree with this statement? **[16]**

Using a case study, assess the relative importance of the different physical factors influencing a landscape shaped by the action of ice sheets **[16]**

Explain the different management strategies taking place in one periglacial landscape you have studied **[16]**

Short Questions:

1. Study **Table 1** which shows inputs and outputs of water for a glacier in Greenland in 2023.

		Summer	Winter
Input (m³)	Wind redistribution	2	15
	Direct snowfall	0	90
	Avalanche	0	140
Output (m³)	Melting	110	5
	Evaporation/sublimation	60	15

Table 1: Inputs and outputs for Greenland glacier 2023

(a) Find the mode(s) of the data set shown in **Table 1**.　　　**[2]**

(b) Calculate the mass balance for each season shown in **Table 1**. You must show your working.　　　**[2]**

(c) state whether each season was in surplus, deficit or equilibrium state.　　　**[2]**

(d) State **two** disadvantages of **Table 1** as a data presentation technique to show inputs and outputs of a glacier system.　　**[2]**

Dryland Landscapes

8 Mark Questions:

Explain the roles of flows of energy in the formation of a Barchan. **[8]**

Explain how polar drylands can be viewed as a system. **[8]**

Explain how geology influences dryland landscape systems. **[8]**

Explain the influence of climate change on pediments. **[8]**

Explain the influence of sediment availability on dryland landscape systems. **[8]**

Explain the role of deposition in the formation of a bajada. **[8]**

16 Mark Questions:

Using a case study, assess the extent to which landforms within a low altitude desert are inter-related. **[16]**

Explain how different physical factors influence the formation of star dunes. **[16]**

'The changes caused by human activity in dryland landscapes are always negative.' Discuss. **[16]**

'Geology is the most significant influence on dryland landscapes.' To what extent do you agree with this statement? **[16]**

Using a case study, assess the relative importance of the different physical factors influencing the landscape of a mid-latitude desert. **[16]**

Short Questions:

1. Study **Table 1** which shows monthly average wind speed for a dryland landscape in Nevada, USA, 2023

Month	Jan	Feb	Mar	Apr	May	Jun	Jul	Aug	Sep	Oct	Nov	Dec
Wind speed (knots)	2	3	6	6	3	7	4	9	9	8	3	3

Table 1: average windspeed Nevada, USA, 2023

(a) Calculate the mean monthly wind speed for the data shown in **Table 1**. You must show your working. **[2]**

(b) Calculate the standard deviation for the data in **Table 1**. You must show your working and give your answer to 2 d.p. **[4]**

(c) Calculate the interquartile range for the data in **Table 1**. You must show your working. **[4]**

(d) Calculate the mode for the data shown in **Table 1**. You must show your working. **[2]**

Earth's Life Support Systems

10 Mark Questions:

Examine the significance of the role of vegetation in linking the water and carbon cycles. **[10]**

Examine how feedback loops can affect the processes and stores within the carbon cycle. **[10]**

Examine the extent to which an individual tree can influence the water and carbon cycles within a tropical rainforest. **[10]**

Examine how water extraction influences flows and stores in the water cycle. **[10]**

Examine the significance of short-term changes to the flows and stores in the water cycle. **[10]**

16 Mark Questions:

'Reducing emissions is the most effective global management strategy to protect the carbon cycle as a regulator of the Earth's climate.' How far do you agree with this statement? **[16]**

Assess the extent to which deforestation and farming affects the water and carbon cycles of a tropical rainforest. **[16]**

Assess the impact of long-term climate change on the water and carbon cycles. **[16]**

"Human factors affect the water cycle more significantly in the tropical rainforest than in the Arctic tundra". Discuss **[16]**

Assess the importance of carbon for humans **[16]**

Assess the importance of water for humans **[16]**

Short Questions:

1. Study **Fig.1**, which shows deforestation in the Amazon rainforest.

(a) Give **three** disadvantages of **Fig.1** to show deforestation. **[3]**

(b) With reference to **Fig.1**, suggest how variation in deforestation will influence carbon storage in the Amazon. **[4]**

Changing Spaces; Making Places

6 Mark Questions:

Explain how people's perception of a place can vary according to their age. **[6]**

Explain how people's perception of a place can vary according to their gender. **[6]**

Explain how people's behaviour and activity in a place can be influenced by their level of emotional attachment to it. **[6]**

Suggest **two** ways that time-space compression can influence our sense of place. **[6]**

Explain **two** ways that different levels of income influence social inequality. **[6]**

Suggest **two** ways that globalisation can influence our sense of place. **[6]**

16 Mark Questions:

How far do you agree that place identity at a local scale is shaped by natural characteristics? **[16]**

'The impact of structural economic change on people and place is mainly socio-economic.' Evaluate this statement in the context of **one** country or region. **[16]**

'Successful rebranding of a place is rarely the product of a single strategy.' To what extent do you agree? **[16]**

To what extent do present day connections shape the identity of a place? **[16]**

'Placemaking is used by governments only to attract inward investment.' How far do you agree with this statement? **[16]**

How would you define a place? **[16]**

Short Questions:

1. Study **Fig.2**, which shows part of Deira City Centre, Dubai, UAE

Fig.2 Deira City Centre, Dubai, UAE

(a) Use **one** piece of evidence from **Fig.2** to explain why local residents might contest efforts to rebrand their neighbourhood.

[3]

(b) Explain why **Fig.2** is an informal representation of a place. [4]

(c) Using evidence from **Fig.2**, compare informal and formal representations of a place. [8]

19

Trade In the Contemporary World

8 Mark Questions:

With reference to an advanced country (AC) **case study**, examine the political factors that explain its advantages for international trade. **[8]**

With reference to one EDC **case study**, explain the current global pattern of its exports. **[8]**

With reference to a **case study**, explain how limited access to global markets is an obstacle to growth and development for low income developing countries (LIDCs). **[8]**

With reference to an advanced country (AC) **case study**, examine the economic factors that explain its advantages for international trade. **[8]**

16 Mark questions:

'The greatest challenges within the global trade system are faced by LIDCs.' Discuss. **[16]**

'Advanced countries benefit the most from the opportunities created by international trade.' How far do you agree? **[16]**

Using a **case study** of **one** EDC, assess the changes in its international trade patterns over time. **[16]**

Using a **case study** of **one** LIDC, explain how political factors have caused it to have limited access to global markets. **[16]**

'Access to markets is only influenced by transport.' To what extent do you agree with this statement? **[16]**

Short Questions:

1. Study **Fig.1** which shows imports of Russian oil into Europe

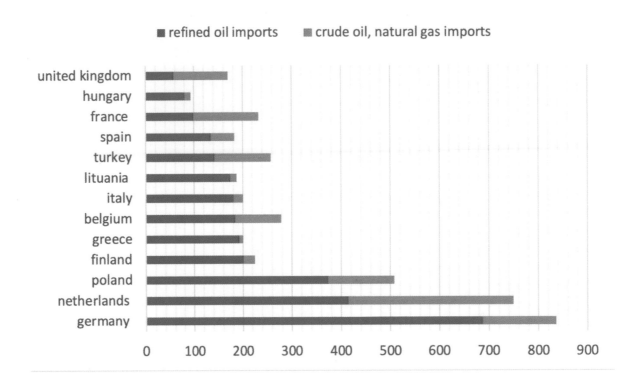

(a) Suggest **two** advantages of the data presentation technique In **Fig.1** for showing variations in imports of Russian oil into Europe. **[4]**

(b) Explain **two** factors which might account for the variation in Imports shown in **Fig.1**. **[5]**

Global Migration

8 Mark Questions:

With reference to an AC **case study**, explain the social challenges caused by international migration. **[8]**

With reference to an emerging and developing country (EDC) **case study**, examine the impact of migration on its economic development. **[8]**

With reference to a **case study**, explain how limited access to global markets is an obstacle to growth and development for low-income developing countries (LIDC). **[8]**

With reference to a **case** study, evaluate the relationship between patterns of international migration and socio-economic development. **[8]**

16 Mark Questions:

'The greatest challenges within the global migration system are faced by LIDCs.' Discuss. [16]

'Advanced countries benefit the most from the opportunities created by international migration.' How far do you agree? [16]

Using a **case study** of **one** EDC, discuss the interdependence with other countries which are connected to the EDC by migrant flows. [16]

Explain how changes in the 21st century have led to a high concentration of young workers and female migrants. [16]

Assess the relationship between patterns of international migration and socio-economic development. [16]

Short Questions:

1. Study **Fig.1** which shows number of immigrants living in the UK by country of birth.

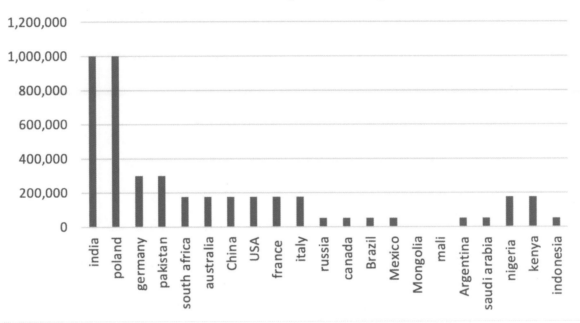

Where Britains immigrants originate from

(a) Suggest **two** ways the number of immigrants living in the UK by country of birth, show in **Fig.1**, can influence flows of money.

[2]

(b) Explain **one** factor which might account for the spatial variations in **Fig.1**.

[3]

Human Rights

8 Mark Questions:

With reference to a **case study** of an **LIDC**, assess the challenges for global governance of human rights. **[8]**

With reference to a **case study** of **one** country, explain the strategies used to address gender inequality issues. **[8]**

With reference to a **case study** of an **LIDC** assess the reasons for the human rights issues taking place. **[8]**

Using a **case study** of one area of conflict, assess the consequences of global governance of human rights for local communities. **[8]**

16 Mark Questions:

'It is the strategies of the UN which offer the most effective protection of human rights in areas of conflict.' To what extent do you agree? **[16]**

'Global governance of human rights issues is of greater consequence for citizens and places in the short term rather than the longer term.' Discuss. **[16]**

'Social factors are the most important influences responsible for gender inequalities.' Discuss. **[16]**

'Level of economic development is the most important influence on maternal mortality rate globally.' Discuss. **[16]**

'Conflict is both a cause and a consequence of human rights violations in areas.' Discuss. **[16]**

Short Questions:

1. Study **Fig.1**, which shows maternal mortality rates for selected countries, 2020

Country	Maternal Mortality Rate 2020 (Maternal deaths per 100,000 live births)
Japan	4
UK	11
USA	24
India	103
Afghanistan	620
Mali	440
South Sudan	1223

(a) Calculate the value of the mean for the data in **Fig.1**.
You must show your working. **[2]**

(b) Give **one** advantage and **one** disadvantage of using the mean to describe this data. **[2]**

(c) Suggest **two** factors which might account for global variation in maternal mortality rates. **[5]**

Power and Borders

8 Mark Questions:

With reference to a **case study** of an **LIDC**, assess the challenges for global governance of **either** sovereignty **or** territorial integrity. **[8]**

With reference to a **case study** of **one** country, explain how challenges to its sovereignty can have impacts on people. **[8]**

With reference to a **case study** of **one** area of conflict, assess the interventions and interactions of organisations taking place. **[8]**

With reference to a **case study** of **one** country, explain how its sovereignty has been challenged. **[8]**

16 Mark Questions:

'The most significant role in regulating the challenge of conflict is fulfilled by the UN.' Discuss. **[16]**

'Global governance of sovereignty issues is of greater consequence for citizens and places in the short term rather than the long term.' Discuss. **[16]**

'For local communities in areas of conflict, intervention can create more problems than it solves.' Discuss. **[16]**

'The most significant role in reproducing the global system of sovereign nation-states is norms.' Discuss. **[16]**

Short Questions:

1. Study **Fig.1**, which shows state fragility index for selected countries,2022

Country/State	State Fragility Index 2022
Germany	23.6
Japan	31
USA	46.6
India	75.3
Mali	98.6
Afghanistan	105.9
South Sudan	108.4

(a) Calculate the value of the mean for the data in **Fig.1.**
   You must show your working.   **[2]**

(b) Give **one** advantage and **one** disadvantage of using the
   mean to describe this data.   **[2]**

(c) Suggest **two** ways that current political boundaries
   might have an influence on the erosion of sovereignty.   **[5]**

Climate Change

Examine how climate change can affect weathering and erosion within any **one** landscape system you have studied. **[12]**

Examine how impacts of climate change can affect informal representations of place. **[12]**

Assess how responses to climate change are affected by issues of **either** human rights **or** territorial integrity. **[12]**

Examine how climate change may be impacting the water cycle in tropical rainforests. **[12]**

Examine how climate change may be impacting the carbon cycle in the Arctic Tundra. **[12]**

33 Mark Questions:

'The vulnerability of people to the impacts of climate change is mainly the result of economic factors.' Discuss. **[33]**

'Physical factors influence climate change more than human factors.' Discuss. **[33]**

'Evidence from the past contributes to accurate predictions of future climate change.' Discuss. **[33]**

'Vulnerability to climate change depends on location rather than the level of economic development.' Discuss. **[33]**

'Changes in anthropogenic greenhouse gas emissions since the pre-industrial era reflect economic development at a national scale.' Discuss. **[33]**

Assess the success of adaptation strategies to reduce the vulnerability of human populations at risk from climate
change. **[33]**

Short Questions:

1. Study **Fig.1** which shows Franz Josef Glacier, New Zealand

(a) Identify **three** limitations of **Fig.1** as a source of information about shrinking ice as a result of climate change. **[3]**

(b) Explain the role and possible bias of the media in shaping the public image of climate change. **[6**

Disease Dilemmas

Synoptic Questions:

Assess how the global distribution of communicable disease is affected by **either** global trade **or** global migration. **[12]**

Examine how the prevalence of non-communicable disease is influenced by issues of **either** human rights **or** territorial integrity. **[12]**

Assess how patterns of diseases are influenced by changes in **one** landscape system you have studied. **[12]**

Examine how disease risks can impact place profiles. **[12]**

33 Mark Questions:

Assess the relative importance of social factors influencing the spread of disease. **[33]**

'Increased global mobility is the most important influence on the spread of communicable diseases.' How far do you agree with this statement? **[33]**

To what extent can **one** NGO effectively mitigate against disease at a national scale? **[33]**

'Increasing mobility is the main influence on diffusion of disease at a variety of scales.' To what extent do you agree? **[33]**

Evaluate the extent to which mitigation strategies can successfully reduce the outbreak and impacts of non-communicable disease. **[33]**

Short Questions:

1. Study **Fig.2** which shows survival rates for common cancers in the UK (2011)

Type of cancer	Survival rates (%)
Prostate (men only)	77
Breast (women only)	75
Cervix	60
Lung	5
Brain	12
Stomach	12
Kidney	50

(a) Identify **three** limitations of **Fig.2** as a source of information about survival rates for common cancers in the UK. **[3]**

(b) Explain cultural causes of non-communicable diseases. **[6]**

(c) Use the data in **Fig.2** to calculate the mode.
You must show your working. **[2]**

Exploring Oceans

Synoptic Questions:

Assess how pollution in oceans is influenced by players driving economic change. **[12]**

Assess how the use of oceans is affected by **either** the global system of trade **or** the global system of migration. **[12]**

Examine how oceans influence patterns of **either** global trade **or** global migration. **[12]**

Assess how the use of oceans is affected by issues of global governance in relation to **either** human rights **or** territorial integrity. **[12]**

Assess ways in which ocean processes influence the carbon cycle. **[12]**

33 Mark Questions:

'Economic factors account for rising levels of oceanic pollution.' Discuss. **[33]**

To what extent does the successful management of oceanic resources require international cooperation? **[33]**

'Adaptations by island communities to the impacts of rising sea levels can be successful.' How far do you agree with this statement? **[33]**

Examine the extent to which oil spills are more damaging to the ocean than the accumulation of plastic? **[33]**

To what extent are oceans hazardous obstacles to human activities? **[33]**

Examine the extent to which the use of ocean energy and mineral resources is sustainable. **[33]**

Short Questions:

1. Study **Fig.1** which shows number of humpback whales in selected ocean areas.

Ocean area	Estimate of Number	Year estimate made
Antarctic	42,000	1997
South-Eastern Pacific	6,200	2005
Off Western Australia	29,000	2008
Off Western Africa	9,800	2005
Western North Atlantic	11,600	1992
Off Western Greenland	2,700	2007
North Pacific	22,000	2007

(a) Identify **three** limitations of **Fig.1** as a source of information about humpback whale populations. **[3]**

(b) Explain variations in nutrient supply within oceans. **[6]**

Future Of Food

Synoptic Questions:

Assess how food security can be affected by issues of **either** human rights **or** territorial integrity. **[12]**

Examine how changes in the global food system have been influenced by time-space compression. **[12]**

Assess how attempts to increase food production can affect water cycles. **[12]**

Examine how physical factors affect food security in any **one** landscape system you have studies. **[12]**

Assess how globalisation of the food industry affects stores in water systems. **[12]**

33 Mark Questions:

'Threats to food security are greatest in dryland areas.' Discuss. **[33]**

'Imbalances in global food production have a greater impact on people than the environment.' Discuss. **[33]**

'Advanced Countries will always experience food security.' To what extent do you agree with this statement? **[33]**

'Food production and food security issues have a greater impact on the physical environment than they do on people.' Discuss. **[33]**

Assess the view that natural shocks are the biggest threat to global food security. **[33]**

To what extent can long-term food security be achieved through local and national initiatives? **[33]**

Short Questions:

1. Study **Fig.1** which shows levels of food security across India.

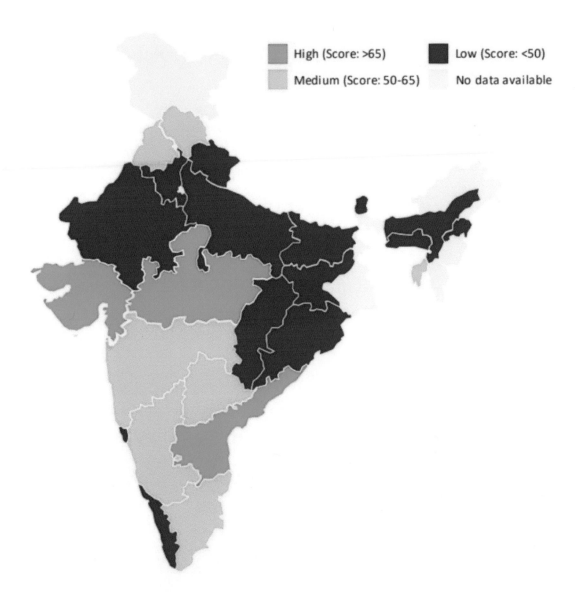

(a) Identify **three** limitations of **Fig.1** as a source of information about food security in India. **[3]**

(b) Explain how feeding the world is a complex system. **[6]**

Hazardous Earth

Examine how impacts of seismic activity are severely worsened by the water cycle. **[12]**

Assess how tectonic hazards impact **either** global trade **or** global migration. **[12]**

Assess how impacts of volcanic eruptions can affect place identity. **[12]**

Examine how strategies to manage tectonic hazards shape place identity. **[12]**

Examine how the risks from tectonic hazards affect place making processes. **[12]**

33 Mark Questions:

Assess the importance of governments in reducing the risks of tectonic hazards over time. **[33]**

'Earthquakes generate only local hazards.' Discuss. **[33]**

'The impacts of tectonic hazards are mainly economic rather than political or environmental.' Discuss. **[33]**

All types of plate boundaries generate tectonic hazards for people. To what extent are those at convergent boundaries the most damaging? **[33]**

'The impacts of earthquake activity vary with levels of economic development.' How far do you agree with this statement? **[33]**

'Over time the ability to manage hazards from volcanic activity increases.' Examine the extent to which this

statement is true. **[33]**

Short Questions:

1. Study **Fig.1** which shows part of the East African Rift Valley

(a) Identify **three** limitations of **Fig.1** as a source of information about rift valleys. **[3]**

(b) Explain the role of convection currents in the asthenosphere. **[6]**

Check out our website!

Phillipsrecources.co.uk

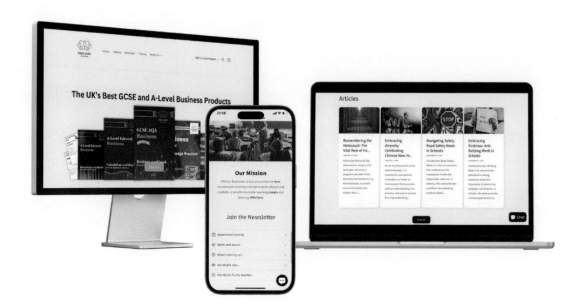

Explore hundreds more resources for all subjects

Printed in Great Britain
by Amazon